SAMUEL BARBER
SOUVENIRS

Op. 28

Ed. 3448

G. SCHIRMER, Inc.

DISTRIBUTED BY

HAL•LEONARD®
CORPORATION

7777 W. BLUEMOUND RD. P.O. BOX 13819 MILWAUKEE, WI 53213

In 1952 I wrote this suite of piano duets to play with a friend. Later I orchestrated it for concert use and several ballet companies have danced it, to various choreographies. Had I myself been choreographer I might have imagined a divertissement in a setting reminiscent of the Palm Court of the Hotel Plaza in New York; the year about 1914, epoch of the first tangos. *Souvenirs* — remembered with affection, not in irony or with tongue in cheek, but in amused tenderness.

S. B.

SAMUEL BARBER

SOUVENIRS

Op. 28

ONE PIANO, FOUR HANDS (Original)
→ PIANO SOLO (Arranged by the composer)
ORCHESTRA (Study Score No. 66)

G. SCHIRMER, Inc.

DISTRIBUTED BY

HAL•LEONARD®

to Charles Turner

Souvenirs

Samuel Barber, Op. 28
Arranged for piano solo
by the composer

I
Waltz

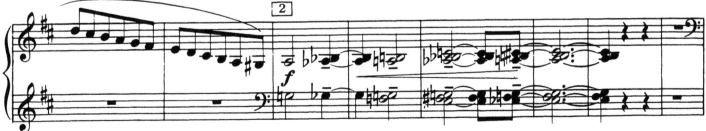

Un poco meno ♩. = 66

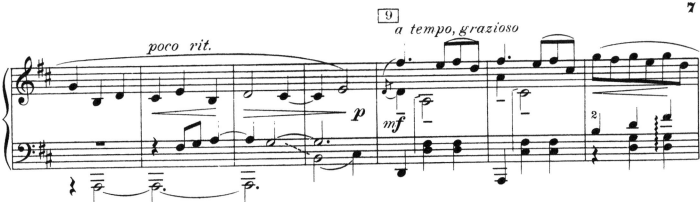

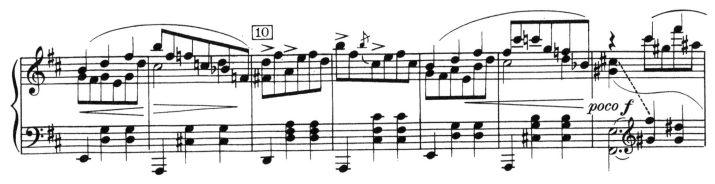

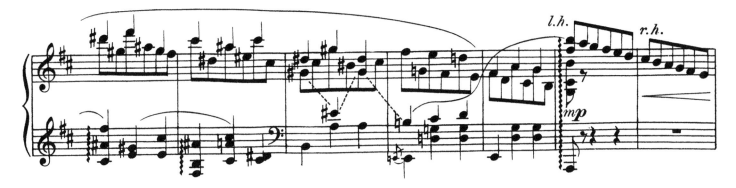

8

II
Schottische

Tempo di Schottische, allegro ma non troppo ♩ = 88

Piano

Doppio mosso, presto

2:30

III

Pas de deux

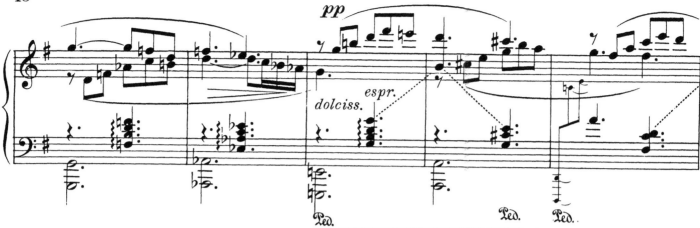

IV

Two-Step

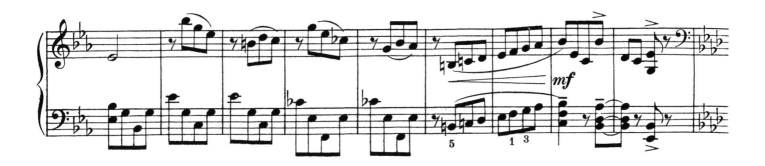

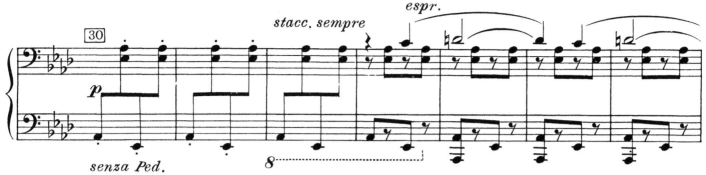

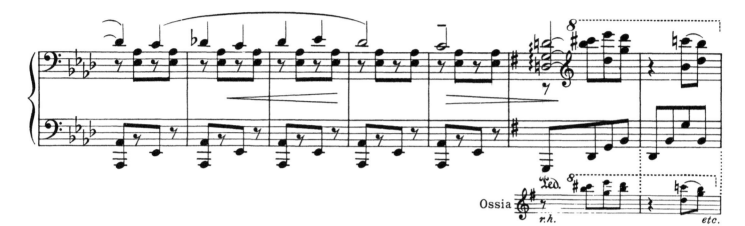

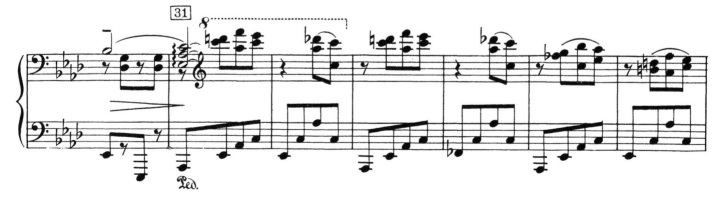

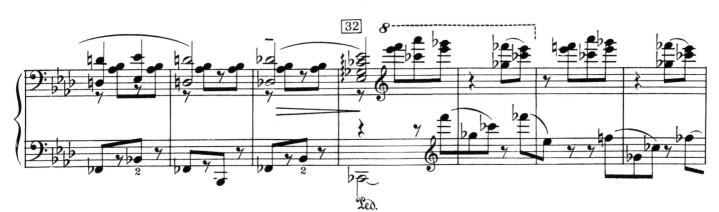

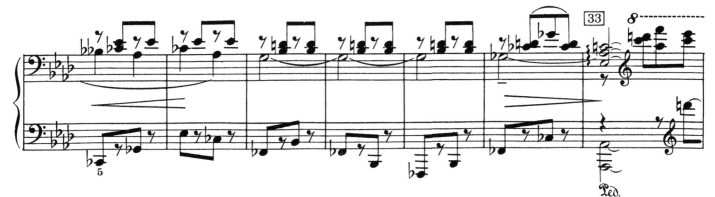

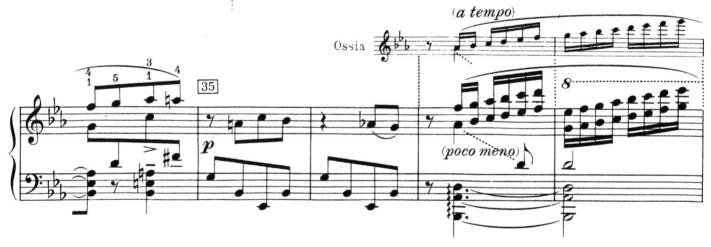

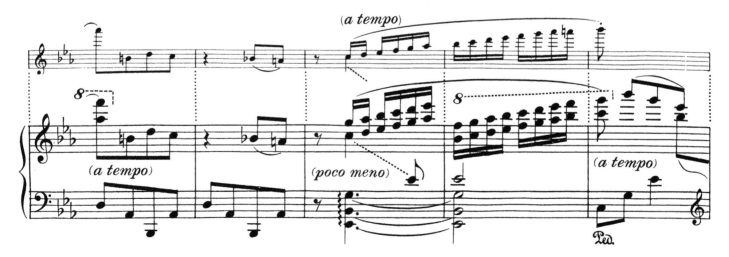

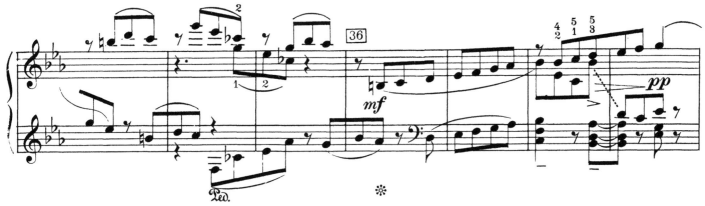

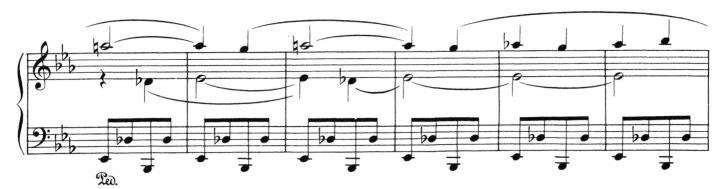

V

Hesitation-Tango

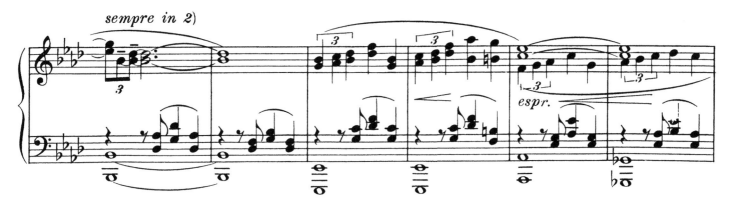

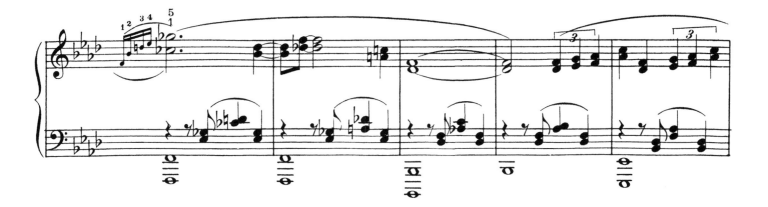

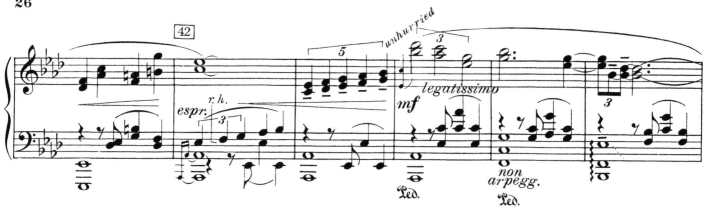

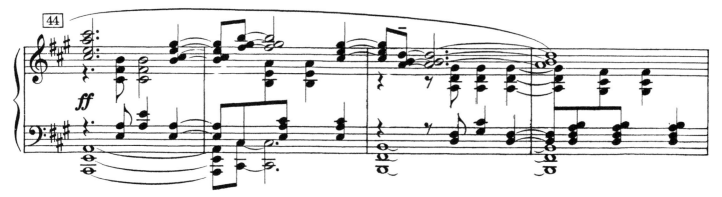

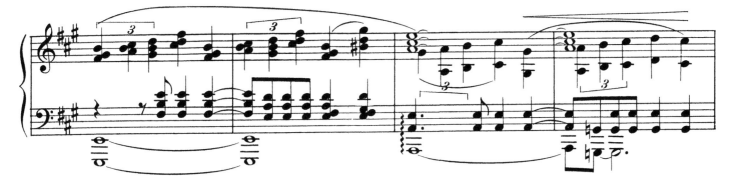

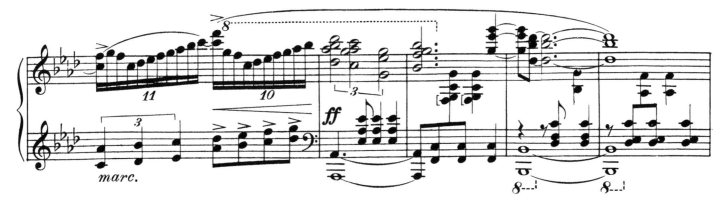

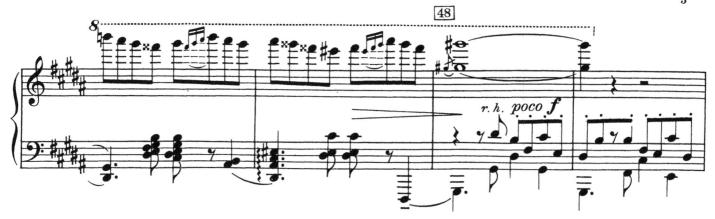

VI
Galop

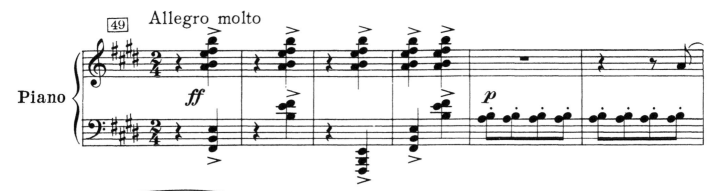

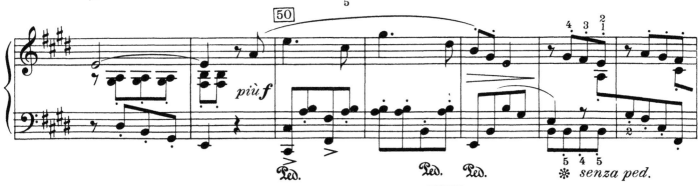

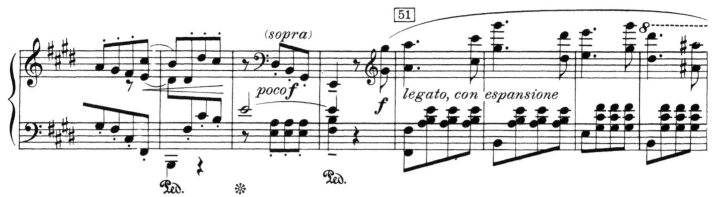

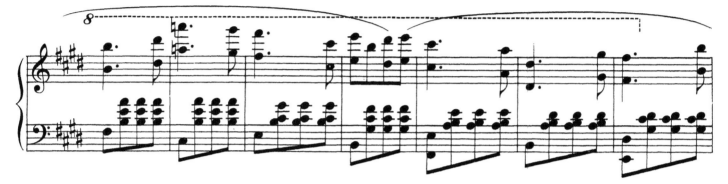

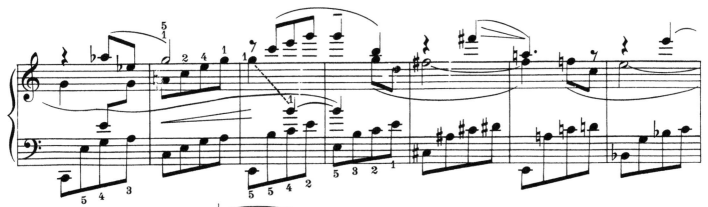

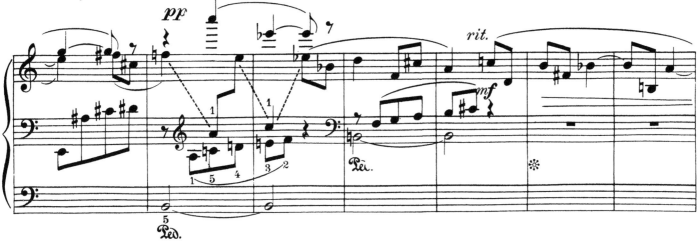

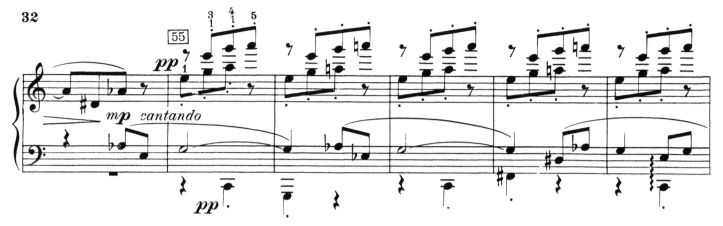

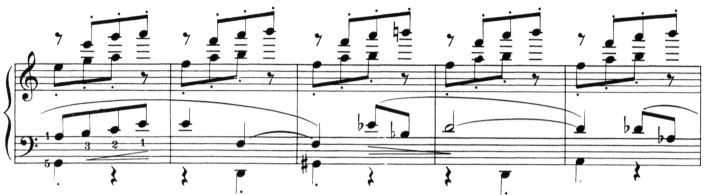

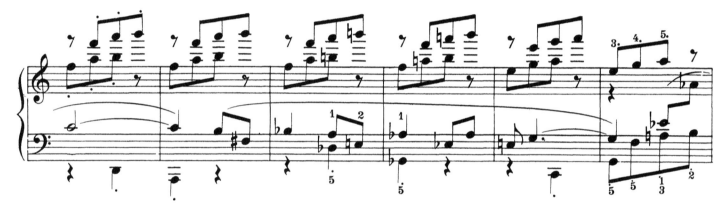

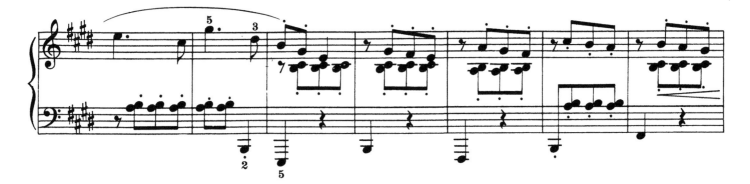

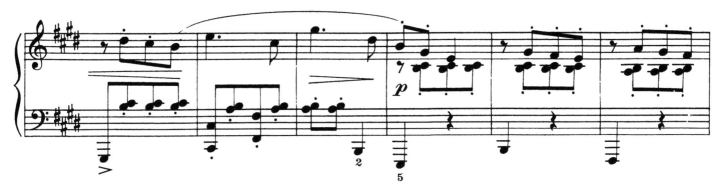

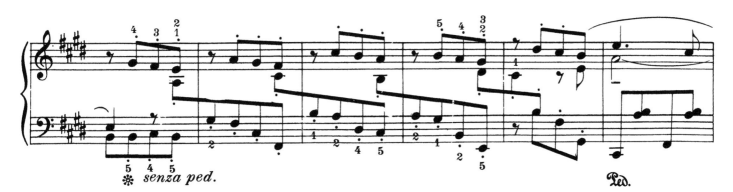

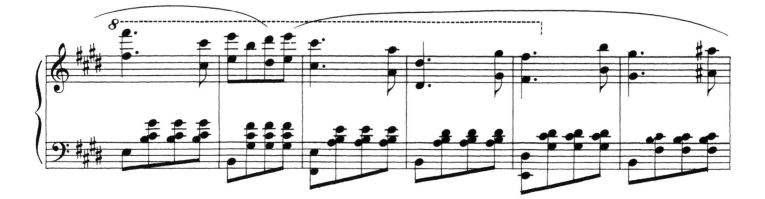